SPIRITS OF
BROKEN DREAMS

The Hauntings of
Beechworth Asylum

ASYLUM
GHOST TOURS

Beechworth, Victoria
www.asylumghosttours.com

SPIRITS OF BROKEN DREAMS
The Hauntings of Beechworth Asylum

© 2020 Asylum Ghost Tours
www.asylumghosttours.com

Research – Dawn Roach
Compilation – Geoff Brown
Cover and Interior Design – Geoff Brown
Cover Image – Dean Samed

Photographers:
Andrew Spedding
p17 by Rinus, CC BY-SA
Danni O'Neill
Some photos and floorplans sourced from
the State Library of Victoria and the
Public Record Office, Victoria.

www.asylumghosttours.com
Mayday Hills Asylum, Beechworth

CONTENTS

BROKEN DREAMS series

Palace of Broken Dreams
(A Brief History of Beechworth Asylum)

Spirits of Broken Dreams
(The Hauntings of Beechworth Asylum)

Upcoming Releases

People of Broken Dreams
(The Patients and Staff of Beechworth Asylum)

INTRODUCTION

Welcome to the world of paranormal investigation and ghost-hunting.

Spirits of Broken Dreams is written as a guide to the hauntings of the infamous Beechworth Asylum in Australia, as well as a basic how-to manual for paranormal investigators... aka ghosthunters.

Through this volume, the second in the *'Broken Dreams'* series, we hope to introduce you to the world we work in, the exciting (and sometimes scary) world of the paranormal.

The world of ghosts.

Belief in ghosts is, at this point, subjective. People who have experienced paranormal phenomena don't need to be convinced, and those who haven't (if they don't want to believe) will likely not be convinced until they do experience something personally. Then everything changes.

There are many sceptics out there, and to be fair, there is no scientific validation of life after death. That's not to say it won't happen; science is ever-evolving, finding new theories. Just because we can't definitively say right now that ghosts do or don't exist and hauntings are real, who's to say what will be discovered in the future.

> *"When I got here I didn't believe in ghosts and spirits, [but] by the time I left I had changed my mind..."*
> –Pete D, Google review for Asylum Ghost Tours – Beechworth

A large portion of the population believes in ghosts to one degree or another. Various polls conducted in the US in 2014 suggest around 45% of Americans believe in ghosts, and a similar survey in the UK at the same time showed that "One in four British people believe that a house can be haunted by some kind of supernatural being, and almost as many (34%) think that ghosts actually exist." It would not be hard to suggest somewhat similar percentages here in Australia.

Parapsychology is the field of study concerned with the investigation of paranormal and psychic phenomena, including telepathy, precognition, clairvoyance, psychokinesis, near-death experiences, reincarnation, apparitional experiences, and, of course, the spirit world. Parapsychology is often called a pseudoscience, due to the application of scientific methodology to study the paranormal world. The equipment we use to hunt ghosts works on well-founded scientific principles, and applies them to theories around the energies that ghosts and spirits may be made up of. The most common thought is that spirits still emit a lot of the same energies emitted by living beings; electromagnetic fields and static electricity. To that end, devices that read those energies are the basic tools of ghosthunters.

Paranormal TV shows have taken a turn upward in popularity in recent years, and horror films based on ghosts and ghost-hunting have certainly helped with that.

Famous investigators like Zak Bagans and Nick Groff of *Ghost Adventures,* and Nick's new series *Paranormal Lockdown,* have certainly helped bring ghost-hunting more into the public eye. Others like Ed and Lorraine Warren, with years of case-files, books, and many recent films based around or linked to their infamous decades of trying to explain the paranormal, have contributed to the popularity as well.

In this book, we'll look at what ghosts could be, how paranormal investigations work (including current equipment and standard techniques) and the spirit world of the Beechworth Asylum, where ghost tours and paranormal investigations take place throughout the year.

We'll look at finding and recording evidence of supernatural encounters, the asylum itself and the spirits known to inhabit the buildings and grounds, and finally, some of the evidence we've collected since we started running tours in late 2015.

If you are interested, you can always come along to Beechworth by booking through Asylum Ghost Tours – Beechworth, who are open most days of the year for various offerings including history tours, ghost tours, and paranormal investigation tours. Sleepover events happen regularly, and sometimes psychic tours as well.

Thank you for purchasing this volume and we hope you enjoy these tales of our ghost-hunting experiences, and feel inspired to go on your own investigation.

Geoff Brown – 2020

WHAT ARE GHOSTS?

According to Wikipedia, "…a ghost (alternatively known as an apparition, haunt, phantom, poltergeist, shade, spectre, spirit, spook, and wraith, along with many other things) is the soul or spirit of a dead person or animal that can appear to the living." For simplicity, we will simply refer to them throughout this narrative as spirits or ghosts.

Stories of spiritual visitations have likely been told since the dawn of humankind, and nearly every recorded culture has a folklore that deals with the appearance of those who stay around the earthly plane after death. Spirits of the dead are likely the most common cross-cultural phenomenon throughout the many eras of mankind.

Throughout history, descriptions of ghosts have ranged from an invisible presence, a barely-visible entity (with or without shape) to the rare and realistic, lifelike visions we call full-body apparitions.

According to our experiences, ghosts may appear in any of these forms, and in the four-plus years since we took over the old Beechworth Asylum, they have. We will cover known apparitions at the asylum in later chapters.

Life-after-death has always fascinated humanity. Religions promise various ways for the soul to remain after the body has passed, and have done for as long as we can remember. In Western society, spiritualists of the 1800s rode a sudden wave of interest in ghosts and life-after-death, with séances and readings performed by mediums claiming to be able to contact or bring forward one's dead relatives. Due to the efforts of sceptics like Harry Houdini and many scientists of the day, most of these performers were found to be fakes, using trickery to produce knockings and disembodied voices from hidden panels in walls or cupboards, and many more of what came to be known as parlour tricks. A favourite of many was the production of ectoplasm from within the body of the medium, most-often shown to be no more than papier-mâché or muslin (or other similar cloth) ingested prior to the beginning of the séance or stage show and regurgitated during a scripted performance.

One well-known practitioner of ectoplasmic trickery was Marthe Beraud, also known as Eva C. and Eva Carrière.

FIGS. 88 AND 89. FLASHLIGHT PHOTOGRAPHS OF 21 MAY, 1912.
LEFT: FIRST PHOTOGRAPH. RIGHT: SECOND PHOTOGRAPH.

IMAGE: In 1920 Carrière was investigated by the Society for Psychical Research in London and an analysis of her ectoplasm revealed it to be made of chewed paper and the ghostly faces as cut from the French magazine *Le Miroir*.

We, at Asylum Ghost Tours, see things differently. For us, ghosts are not parlour tricks.

Ghosts are also not things that can be explained by our current knowledge of science, but that may well change in the future.

The most common understanding seems to be that ghosts are those who choose to stay behind (or are left behind) after their time on Earth is up. Some may have unfinished business, some may be scared of where they are going due to their belief system, and some may not even know they have passed on.

There are many different thoughts on the reasons some disembodied spirits remain; however, paranormal investigators generally agree on two different kinds of hauntings:

1 – Intelligent hauntings: where the ghosts are aware of the people who are around them and interact with them in real time. The spirit may or may not know they have passed on, and may be aware that time has passed or not be aware of the passing years and may see us in their time. This can also include poltergeist-style hauntings, where objects and surroundings are manipulated by hidden energies, although there are other theories around those as well, such as latent psychokinetic abilities (moving objects with the mind) of those hounded by poltergeists.

2 - Non-intelligent (or residual) hauntings: where a spirit or spiritual/emotional echo continues to perform some action or event that occurred in a certain area. These can be the result of a traumatic or memorable action or event that is absorbed by the surroundings, where the spirit of a person is stuck repeating the same thing over and over.

This kind of haunting can also be something other than a person. It could be a sound repeated at a certain time in the same area at particular times. A well-known haunted site in Melbourne has had rumours of a music box being heard just around midnight by many different people for many years now. It could be as complex as the residual energy of the many children known to have lived and died at the site, or it could just be a nearby ice-cream truck as others suggest, although I don't know why an ice-cream truck would be around at midnight. Except on those really long, hot nights in the middle of summer. Then, we all could do with some ice-cream.

The most commonly-held belief of ghosts resides within the known make-up of life and matter on this planet, and the accepted science that energy never dissipates, that it just changes form. Living things contain energies, and if we were to accept (as mainstream science does) that energy can never just disappear, then something must happen to those energies when we pass on. Paranormal investigators believe that the energy of life sometimes remains behind to create the ghosts we investigate, either with awareness or without.

Some famous images of ghosts are included throughout this book, as well as in a longer section at the end, with brief outlines of the situations. We also tell of a few renowned cases investigated by parapsychologists or ghosthunters.

No matter what your belief and where in the spectrum of religion and parapsychology it sits, a large proportion of people throughout the world believe in some form of life-after-death.

One of the most famous ghost images ever taken, this is allegedly the ghost of Lady Dorothy Townshend, who lived in Raynham Hall in Norfolk, England during the 1700s. After her death, Townshend's spirit was reportedly seen many times, and in 1936, a photograph of the interior of Raynham Hall showed this anomoly.

WHAT MAKES A PARANORMAL INVESTIGATION?

Paranormal investigators, also referred to as ghost hunters, generally investigate phenomena pertaining to ghosts and other unexplainable occurrences or beings, including the cryptids (mythical beasts) such as Yowies, Bigfoot, and the Loch Mess Monster. This group of investigators may also include members of sceptic organisations, looking to debunk the phenomena using current science.

Recorded paranormal research dates back to the late 19th century, with a fast-growing interest in contacting those who passed beyond the veil being supported by a fast-growing industry of mediums, psychics, showmen, and sceptics.

The first renowned modern investigator of the paranormal world, Charles Hoy Fort, was the founder of the Fortean Society, a group of paranormal-interested friends from the upper echelons of society within the United States, who investigated and theorised about things that had no scientific explanation, including ghosts and spirits of the dead and departed. The magazine *Doubt* was released by the Fortean Society through until 1959.

Worldwide interest was shown in the matter of spirituality, with organisations such as the UK Society for Psychical Research investigating spiritual matters. Psychic researcher Harry Price published his *Confessions of a Ghost-Hunter* in 1936.

Modern paranormal investigators use physics as well as psychics to hunt ghosts. With the influx of inexpensive equipment that can read the various environmental changes believed to show the presence of spirits, it's not hard to build a basic ghost-hunting kit (as spoken of in detail further on in the book).

Investigators go out (with proper permissions and safety concerns covered) to allegedly-haunted locations in areas they can reach. Some stick in their own cities or regions, while others can travel nationally or even internationally to investigate the more (and less) famous haunted locations.

Every suburb has at least one. An old, abandoned house, a closed-down factory, a disused train tunnel, or sewer tunnels that are no longer part of the system. Something rumoured to be haunted, or the lair of some deadly, undiscovered beast. It's something most of us grew up with.

At this point, I will say that some locations are too dangerous to try to gain entry, particularly tunnels or underground areas. Never place yourself at risk without fully checking out the risks and hazards involved in any exploration. The areas that appear the most interesting are, by their very nature, usually the most dangerous.

The aim of the paranormal professional is to safely explore these abandoned locations and try to investigate the potential for hauntings.

Some use equipment of various standards, and others just use their own senses, or a combination of both.

Let's be straight. The best pieces of equipment a paranormal investigator can use are their own body and senses. Nothing beats seeing, feeling, smelling or hearing something paranormal. Something you know could not possibly have happened. This, however, provides no recorded evidence to convince others of the phenomena.

This technique is most often used by thrill-seekers who are not as dedicated to the area of paranormal investigation as other, more well-equipped groups.

The increase in interest and experimentation by groups worldwide over the last decade or two has led to some fairly well-established equipment for investigators to set up their own basic ghost-hunting kit.

Some of this equipment already existed, and has been re-purposed for use in ghost-hunting, while more recently other pieces have been designed specifically for the concept of finding spirits, finding new means of utilising existing technologies that match the current accepted beliefs on what works and what doesn't to measure and record paranormal experiences.

Ask any paranormal investigator or start a question in a social media group, and most investigators will give you a basic list of equipment with which to begin.

Collecting lists of this kind I have seen over the years, I would suggest the following as a very basic requirement for any budding paranormal investigator:
- a pocket or head-mounted torch,
- a small digital recorder,
- something to read temperature (most people tend towards the laser thermometers used by the catering industry for this, as these allow the testing and comparison of specific areas within a space),
- a notepad to record findings and events, and;
- an adventurous spirit needed to creep around older, haunted places in the dark.

This basic list is the bare essentials you need to conduct and record an investigation.

Add to that the need to let someone know where you're going in case of trouble or injury (as well as what time you expect to return, and the advice to NEVER go alone. Always take someone with you. Sometimes, with the kind of places keen ghost-hunters decide to explore, you may well find homeless people, drug users, gangs of teenagers, or just other (sometimes alcohol-affected) urban explorers out for a jaunt. Such meetings do hold some level of potential danger at times, so make sure you take this into account at all times.

BEFORE YOUR PARANORMAL INVESTIGATION BEGINS

The whole concept of becoming a paranormal investigator isn't as simple as some books, films, or people would have you believe. There are basic rules for safety and for legalities that we really recommend you follow.

Before you go out on the actual investigation, there are many things to do in preparation to try and ensure the result of your expedition has the best possible outcome. Without proper preparation, or the seven 'P's, as I call it, the end results of your investigation may well be underwhelming.

The seven 'P's are: proper preparation and planning prevents piss-poor performance, a saying taken from the British Army, and suitable to anything you're planning to do in life, including paranormal investigations.

Plan, research, prepare, and then conduct the very best investigation you can.

Learn how to use your equipment correctly. It's no use thinking you have set your digital recorder to work and then find at the end of a long night that you needed to have a memory card you didn't take into account. Practise using your equipment to get the outcomes you want. Test and then test again. Make sure you keep detailed lists of all you want to take along, and double (or even triple) up on consumables.

Check your batteries, take spare rechargeable cells, and if your equipment accepts both kinds of batteries, take some spare disposables along in case your original rechargeable batteries are drained a lot quicker than you thought they would be. It happens, trust me.

Check your list. Check it twice. There's nothing worse than driving for three hours to get to your potentially-haunted location to discover you've left the thermos full of coffee (or slab of Monster drinks) back in the kitchen, ready to be packed but somehow left behind.

RESEARCH THE LEGALITY

Okay, you've heard all the rumours, either from locals or online, about some really cool place that is supposed to be haunted. You've decided to go and explore the old house or factory or facility. The first thing you should do is Google. Find out, if you can, who the owners are. The one thing you should NEVER do is enter somewhere illegally. That can lead to a whole heap of problems for your safety, or your wallet in the form of fines for trespass.

Under no circumstances should you just go and break in to some apparently deserted old building. You could end up either in personal danger from other people inside the facility, such as squatters or homeless people (not saying homeless are dangerous, but there is that crossover of homelessness and mental illness to consider), drug-users who are looking for an inconspicuous place to use their substance of choice, or just a group of drunken louts out for a laugh. You don't want to put yourself into danger unnecessarily.

The other potential issue is finding yourself in handcuffs and the back of a police car for break-and-enter and/or trespass, if a neighbour happens to see you entering somewhere you're not supposed to be. The fines and potential gaol-time far outweigh the potential fun of an illegal ghost-hunt.

RESEARCH THE HISTORY

To really understand a haunting, and the results of any investigation, as well as undertaking a good investigation, knowledge of the history of the place you are in is invaluable.

If you just go into somewhere you believe may be haunted, you won't be able to ask the right questions to properly evaluate any answers you may receive.

Find out as much as you can about the site, the building, the land it's built on, and any names of ownership. Find out about the people who lived, worked, and even died there. Find out about any tragedies that may have occurred on the site, within the current building, and also within any other building that may have existed on the site previously. Go back as far as you can, even to the point of finding out if there are any known massacres of natives by colonists that may have taken place on or near the site, or whether it's an Indigenous sacred site with overtones of the Dreamtime spirituality (if you do find there is an Indigenous link, please, please, please contact the local tribal co-op and talk to them about your plans. You don't want to disturb a sacred site purely for fun. As well as being disrespectful, it's just wrong).

The more history you discover before you go, the more forearmed you are for interaction with any entities that may be willing to talk to you.

DRESSING TO IMPRESS

First up, investigators need to dress appropriately for their explorations.

Cool and warm weather certainly both need to be taken into consideration, but the main thing is personal safety.

During summer, it might feel comfortable to wear shorts and thongs (flip-flops if you're American) most of the time, but the level of safety provided by these minimalist items leaves a lot to be desired. We certainly recommend safety over comfort, and when hunting ghosts in run-down places, thongs and shorts leave too many open skin areas to be torn by nails, dropped boards, spikes, broken glass and other hazards, all of which are commonly found in decrepit buildings or areas.

During winter, it may well be nice and warm in your home, but just remember the places you're hunting ghosts are most likely unoccupied, and without any form of heating. Dress in a couple of layers that can be taken off or put on if needed, and always keep a warm jacket and maybe some thin gloves ready in the car for if the night gets colder.

Denim jeans give you a layer of thick cotton protection in case of tumbles or trips, and also help retain warmth.

Finally, work boots, or at the very least, safe and comfortable sealed footwear with soles that grip (like runners), are a necessity.

FINAL CHECKLIST:

1. Never alone.

2. Let someone know what you're doing and where tou're doing it.

3. Take all legal precautions in regard to proper permissions for entry.

4. Dress appropriately.

5. Always carry a phone to call for help if something untoward happens.

6. Carry ID in case someone reports you to the authorities.

7. Research before you go, and memorise as much basic info as you can. Carry the rest in a notebook.

EQUIPMENT

I n this section, we'll look at each of the pieces of equipment we
have that are used during our own paranormal investigations,
outline what each one does, and how each relates to the
theory of hauntings and spirits – both intelligent and residual.

Note: When investigating, always consider false positives
and interference with instruments, especially EMF readers and
fluctuations of temperature. Electricity and phones can give
false readings, so it is always best to turn most phones to flight
mode during the investigation. For safety's sake, and to remain
in contact with the outside world, maybe consider having one
member of the team with an active phone but keep them away
from the meters, and take into account potential interference
when they are near.

It's always a good idea to form a baseline environmental
reading of the area on arrival, to establish the norms of those areas
being investigated. That way, abnormalities can be observed
without being fooled by things that can be explained. This is
especially important where electricity and other environmental
effects are present.

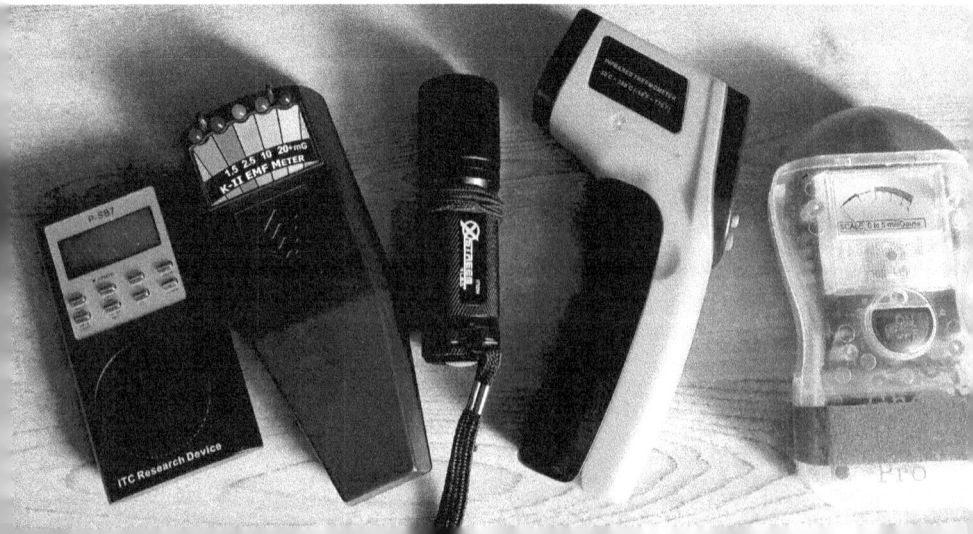

ENVIRONMENTAL CUE EQUIPMENT

Environmental cues involve the many physical and electrical stimuli within our environments. These may include temperature and electromagnetic frequencies, light and shadow, sound waves and other elements of our surroundings.

There are many varied pieces of equipment that register and read these various environmental cues and inform the paranormalist (yes, that now should be a word) of any changes within the environment that may signal some kind of paranormal presence or activity.

We'll list a few of the most common and most commonly-used pieces of equipment, especially those we use ourselves and can speak of with experience.

Dowsing Rods

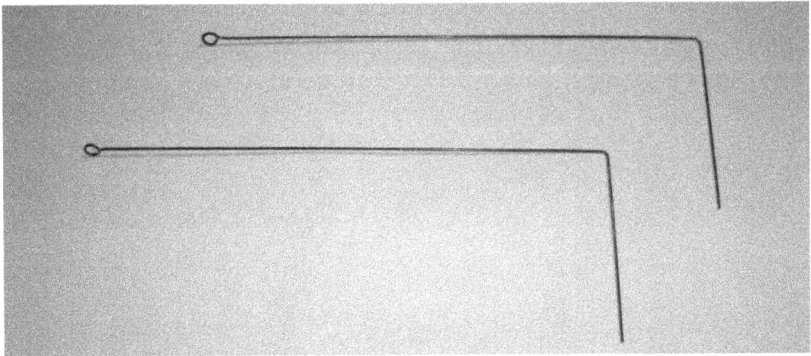

According to Wiki, dowsing is "a type of divination employed in attempts to locate ground water, buried metals or ores, gemstones, oil, gravesites, and many other objects and materials without the use of scientific apparatus". People also use these rods for contacting spirits.

One Y-shaped or two L-shaped rods are usually used for dowsing, which is also known as divining, although some dowsers don't use rods of any kind, preferring to utilise their own senses to feel the energies dowsing rods may detect.

We use the two L-shaped rods here at AGT, one rod held at rest in each hand. When both rods point outward, parallel to each other, and away from you, this is the 'clear' position. When the rods move and cross each other to form an 'X', energy of some kind is detected. Another option we have seen used for communication is to ask for both rods to cross/swing one way for 'yes' and move apart/swing the opposite way for 'no' when answering closed questions.

Electromagnetic frequency is the commonly-held theory of what dowsing-rods (and other equipment) most likely detect while ghost-hunting, although static electricity is also a potential signifier. In the end, dowsing is not scientifically-verified, but certainly seems to work for some people, and has throughout the ages.

Because we don't understand what exact environmental cue this technique utilises, we have placed this at the top of the list, and not within any particular grouping below.

Infra-Red Laser Temperature Gauge

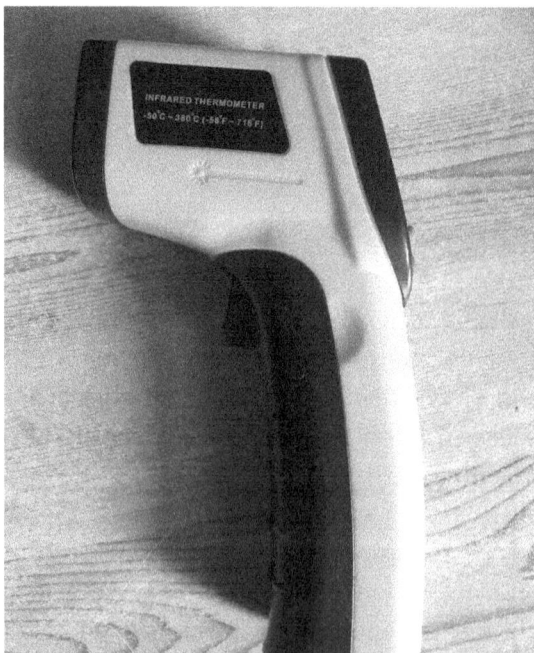

IR laser temperature units, and other means of measuring temperatures within a certain area, are thought to show paranormal activity due to the strongly-held belief that spirits can use heat energy to manifest. The renowned 'cold spot' theory suggests an entity is present, especially if the readings drop more than five degrees below the recorded baseline of the area where the phenomenon is manifesting.

The most commonly used laser gauges are designed for kitchens to measure temperatures of meat by shining an IR laser onto the area requiring measurement and the unit shows the results on a backlit screen, making for easy temperature readings. They measure in Celsius or Fahrenheit with a fair range provided for. These units are found easily in homeware shops or online sites, for less than fifty dollars.

EM (Electromagnetic) Equipment

As Wiki tells us, "an electromagnetic field (also EMF or EM field) is a physical field produced by electrically-charged objects. It affects the behaviour of charged objects in the vicinity of the field. The electromagnetic field extends indefinitely throughout space and describes the electromagnetic interaction. It is one of the four fundamental forces of nature."

There is a variety of paranormal investigation equipment used, which work on the concept of spirits emitting or using electricity in one of its many forms. Many investigators believe the spirits require energy to interact within our reality, explaining that the regularly-reported cold spots in allegedly-haunted locations are a result of the spirits using the thermal energy to create other effects, at the same time lowering the temperature in one place.

Everything that has mass can potentially produce EMF energy. Biomass (living creatures) has been shown to produce EMF (although the peak of radiation we give off is in the infrared, we give off lots of radiation at around 100 GHz (~ 1 millimetre wavelength) and as noted earlier, one paranormal theory suggests that, as science has shown energy can never dissipate but only change form, that energy continues on in the spirit realm.

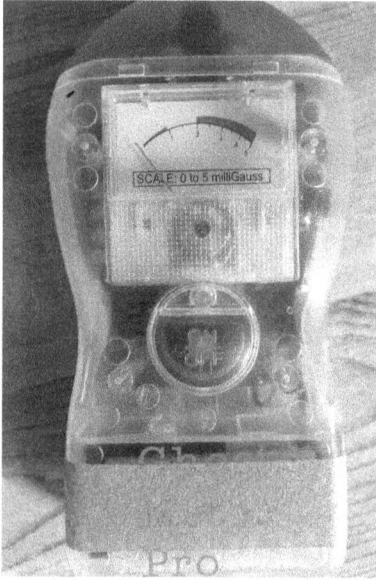

GHOST METER PRO™   KII EMF METER

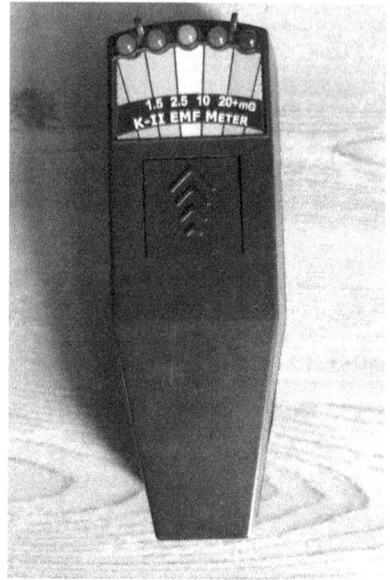

Paranormal investigators also use equipment to produce EM energy. EM pumps are devices specifically designed to create and send out electromagnetic energy to help energise the spirits and make it easier for them to interact with and affect what we can see, hear, feel, and otherwise sense. The theory here is that building the EM energy in a space allows for more frequent and stronger interaction by any entities that use this energy to manipulate the environment around them.

To read EM energy: EMF meters are considered by many para people as the main base-meter for any investigation. They come in many various designs and sensitivities, from ones sold for electricians to use to find live wires inside walls to those designed by ghosthunters for ghosthunters.

Following are some of the most commonly-used devices.

1. Ghost Meter Pro™

The Ghost Meter Pro™ (GMP) detects electromotive force, and alerts you to changes in presence for potential communication with an entity.

There are four various modes on the GMP, but through our own practise and experimentation, we've found the only ones of use to us are modes 3 and 4.

Mode 3 is a normal EMF Gauss meter mode. In this mode the meter is a normal Gauss meter and it looks for EMF (low and radio frequency.) Sometimes, in areas and buildings where power is still present, these fields can be power lines and mobile phones, hence the need explained earlier to set baselines prior to an investigation.

Mode 4 – Communication Mode: answers yes and no questions (closed questions) using lights and sound. According to the manufacturer, "… this sophisticated mode uses filtering to detect patterns that signal harmonics representing coupling, echoing and resonance." To be honest, the circuit boards within the GMP don't really show how this is done, and the device itself certainly doesn't seem to have a set pattern programmed in as some people claim, but we have found this to be the most productive and responsive mode of all, especially once the entities become used to how this mode functions. We have personally observed the same answers to the same questions in the same areas of Mayday Hills, given at different times of day or night and in differing question order. This strengthens for us that we are really communicating with intelligent entities.

2. The Rook™

The Rook™, an EMF device created by Ghoststop in the US, detects small changes in electromagnetic energy and alerts with lights and sound. This detector is specifically designed for ghost-hunting with an emphasis on detecting energy changes and proximity so you can be alerted to a presence and track down the source easily. This device is less sensitive than a GMP, but more sensitive than a KII (outlined below).

3. KII EMF Meter

Used to detect stronger spikes in electromagnetic energy. These spikes are indicated by the multi-coloured lights at the top of the meter, and barring environmental interference, may signify activity or communication from spirits from the other side. Again, a baseline reading from the areas when you first start can help you work out which readings are normal and which are abnormal.

During our time here at Mayday Hills, we have found the KII to be much less responsive than a GMP or Rook most of the time, and when it does register, it is usually a much stronger electromagnetic field than either of the other meters show.

4. Mel Meter

The Mel Meter combines two of the environmental readers into one unit, and offers single axis AC magnetic field measurement and real-time air temperature readings on the

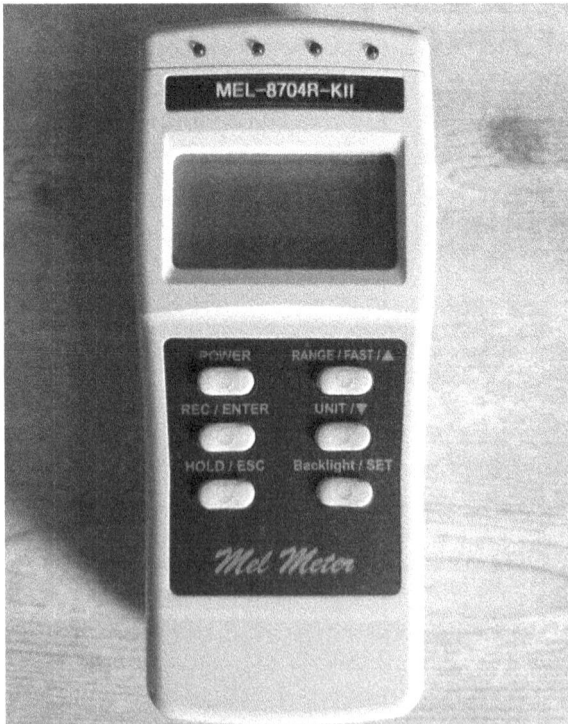

same screen. This allows for correlation between two different environmental cues showing potential paranormal activity on more than one level.

Gary Galka, an electrical engineer who owned a company which developed and built meters for tradesmen and builders, tragically lost his daughter Melissa in a car accident. After some experiences he had that seemed too focused and specific for him to believe it to be anything but paranormal contact, he developed what he called the 'Mel Meter' to try and communicate with Melissa. This piece of equipment is now used worldwide by paranormal investigators.

5. Parascope/Paranologies equipment

A recent manufacturer of paranormal equipment, Paranologies has really leapt into the market.

Using 3D printing, paranologies brings out unique and well-thought-out ways of incorporating old tech into new devices. The main paranologies piece we use at the moment is called a

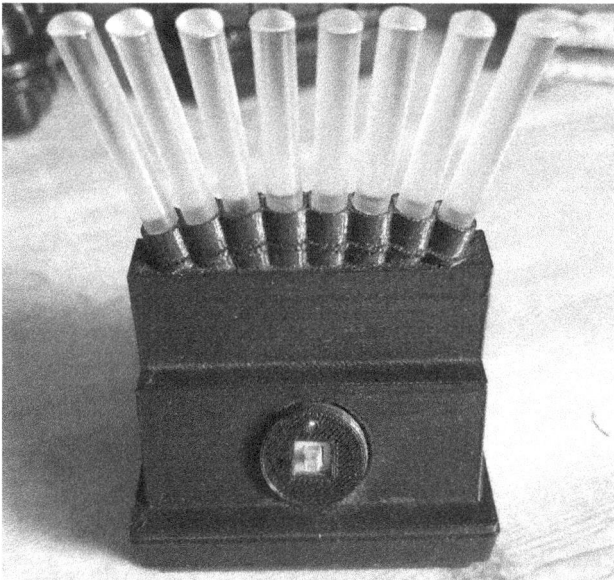

Parascope. The device reads 'triboelectric' (static electricity) fields, using clear rods that light up to show the movement (if

any) of those fields. We find the Parascope to be a brilliant piece of tech, and will be sourcing more and more of the new stuff this innovative company brings out. Later in 2020, we have arranged to source individual units our guests can use themselves, but for now we have one or two Parascopes (dependent on what other tours are running) per group of investigators going through the asylum.

In the early 1960s, the Reverend K.F. Lord photographed the interior of his church in Newby, North Yorkshire, U.K. When the film was developed, a translucent hooded figure appeared to be standing to the right of the altar.

AUDIO AND VISUAL EQUIPMENT

Visual and audio confirmation of paranormal events can be some of the most impressive evidence you can gather. If we had a dollar for every person who asks if they will *see* or *hear* a ghost on our tours, we could buy the remaining portions of the asylum. Humans have five (scientifically-accepted) senses (even though many of us believe we have at least one more) but vision and sound are always our main ones.

Even though evidence of paranormal events can be smelled, felt, or even tasted, everyone wants to see or hear some paranormal activity.

1. Full Spectrum Cameras/Video Recorders
Cameras and video recorders are a very important part of any investigation where you want to be able to analyse and present visual evidence afterwards, rather than just experience the act of investigation.

The cameras that come on the newer mobile phones are of an amazing quality nowadays, and can give us some very interesting results when used, but to really be able to see better what is happening around you during an investigation, there are many infra-red (IR) or full-spectrum (FS) cameras available on the market for reasonable prices. These vary from digital SLR and video cams that that have been adapted to view in spectrums other than those used in normal photography (a simple process, really, of opening the case and removing a specific filter within the camera) to action cams (first designed for sports, most

commonly known as GoPros and their many clones) that have undergone the same adaptation. These action cams are most easily used, and can be mounted anywhere you like with any of the various GoPro mounting systems, from head straps, chest mounts and bike mounts (not really relevant) to general mounts and removable adhesive. After a few minutes, you even forget they are there at times, and they film wherever you are facing for at least 4-5 hours. Just remember to make sure the memory card is large enough for your needs and to carry a replacement battery for the unit.

2. Night Vision Goggles (NVG)

Night vision infra-red devices have long been used by people needing to see in minimal light. The devices have mostly been used by hunters, police or security forces, and the military, for

obvious reasons. More recently, the added ability to see extra light frequencies without having obvious light has brought these viewers into the realm of paranormal investigations. They have their own IR emitters of varying ranges, and the ability to allow the user to 'see' with lenses and such. Some also have memory cards to allow photographs and video to be stored.

The units range in quality and price from mid-three figures for basic hunting units with a monocular setup and a range of a hundred metres, up to hundreds of thousands of dollars for the latest generation military tech with binocular vision and multiple lenses. Of course, these units are most often way too expensive for hobbyists, or even most professional ghost hunters.

Some tour companies are also known to use basic toy IR-vision units that were prevalent on the kid's market last decade, designed as toys for 'spy kids' and selling for as little as fifty to a hundred dollars. These gadgety-type units have a range of around ten metres, which can be suitable for some smaller areas and buildings, but are useless when used in larger facilities.

The hunting units we use for our tours at Mayday Hills are a digital night vision monocular with 4x magnification and 2x digital zoom. They can take photos and video of what the devices are 'seeing', and can be used day or night (daytime vision shows as full-colour with IR switched off, whole night vision is reduced to the greens of IR). They have built-in infrared night vision for long distance viewing up to 100 metres away, which works well in the long corridors and rooms of Mayday Hills. Manual focusing is done using the rotary control on the lens.

3. Laser Grid

Laser grids emit a grid of coloured dots which are useful for detecting movement and shadow phenomena, or general visual activity, during an investigation. You can adjust the size and spread of the dots emitted by twisting the adjustable lens at the front of the unit, and if you detach the lens entirely it functions as a laser pointer.

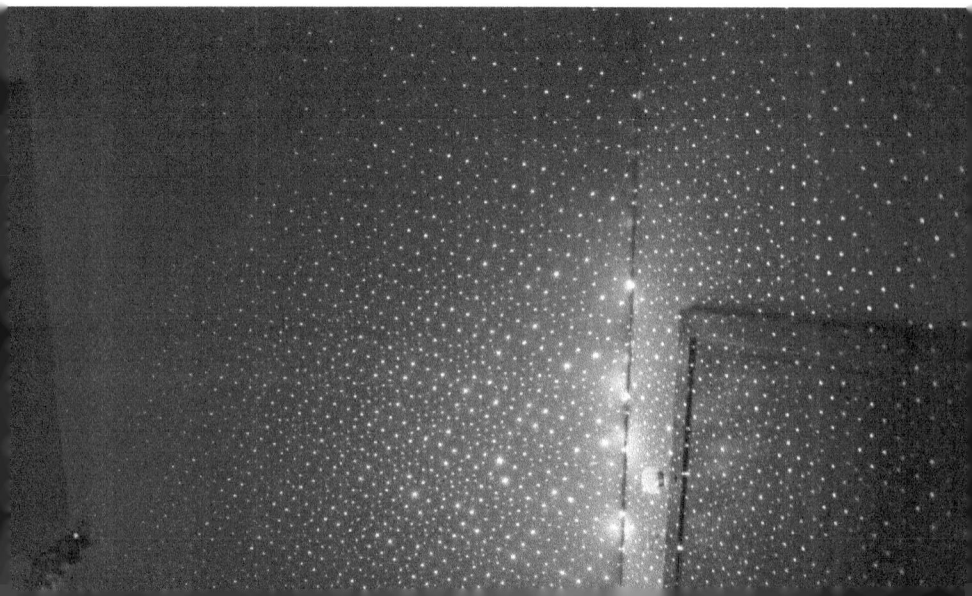

There are various kinds of laser grids available on the market, including the basic ones that are best only used for 5-10 minutes at a time to avoid burnout to the more rugged specialist units with built-in fans so they can be left running for a lot longer. It's best to use one that runs from its own power source rather than the larger and stronger 240v units, as you never know if electricity is available at any particular investigation site.

4. Analog or Digital Recorders

Electronic voice phenomena, or EVP, is an instance of a human voice from an unexplainable source found on recording equipment.

Our research has found many opinions on EVP and using them in the best ways to record potential otherworldly attempts at communication. Many investigators suggest there are two types of EVP – those able to be heard by the human ear (humans averagely hear frequencies from 20 Hz up to 20,000 Hz, although as we get older, the upper limit decreases due to ongoing damage from loud sounds throughout our lives) as well as able to be recorded, and those EVPs outside the range of human hearing that only turn up on the more sensitive recording systems.

There are two types of recording equipment that can be used for this investigation tool; digital recording and analogue recording. At the same time there is much discussion around which is most suitable for recording EVPs.

The differences between the two types are:

Analogue can be more expensive and more complicated. With this kind of recording, a soundwave is recorded directly onto a tape or other recording devices in its original form.

Digital is more easily done. This kind is recorded by adapting and condensing the analogue soundwave into a series of numbers that are then stored on the digital device, which can then be read by equipment to replicate the sounds recorded rather than hearing the sounds themselves.

Digital is easy and cheap these days, whether using a recording app on your mobile phone or an inexpensive digital recorder that are easily and cheaply found on eBay. Analogue simply requires a tape recorder, or even an old minidisc recorder, which has a massive range of frequency recording available.

Both methods of recording EVPs have pros and cons, so for anyone interested in following up on this aspect of paranormal investigation, it may be an idea to have both kinds of recorders running in conjunction to cover all potential frequencies and options. Who knows what might turn up on one, the other, or even on both.

In 1916, retired Scotland Yard Inspector Arthur Springer took this picture in Tingewick, Buckingham, England. At the moment he captured the photograph, there was reportedly no dog in the frame at all.

ITC EQUIPMENT

Instrumental Trans-communication (ITC) is a part of investigations that is becoming more and more common with the drop in prices of the required equipment.

Although ITC can also be considered to include EVP recording equipment, I chose to include that one above and will focus on two pieces of equipment that have risen in popularity recently.

The concept of using modern technology to talk to the dead isn't that modern at all. In the early 1940s, American photographer Attila von Szalay worked with author Raymond Bayless to try and record disembodied voices using first a 78rpm record, with little success. It was only after he moved to a reel-to-reel tape recorder, he started to collect some results he claimed he couldn't explain.

Then, Latvian psychologist Konstantin Raudive published his own experiments and findings in *Breakthrough: An Amazing Experiment in Electronic Communication with the Dead* in 1968, which was translated and republished in English in 1971.

In 1980, William O'Neal first constructed his Spiritcom, built to plans he claimed he psychically received from George Mueller, a scientist six years dead, with some claimed results showing communication with spirits using the device.

Then, in 2002, paranormal-interested Frank Sumption created the renowned Spirit Box/Frank's Box using plans he claimed to have received from the spirit world.

The equipment has grown and developed since those days, and there are specific items and devices more commonly used than others.

1. Spirit Box

An often-used piece of equipment for communication is the Spirit Box/Ghost Box or Frank's Box, with the most common being the Spirit Box 7 or P-SB7.

There is the more modern P-SB11 now making its way into

more para kits, but the P-SB7 is still the most common, and they still do the same thing. The P-SB7 uses radio-frequency sweeps to generate white noise through an integrated speaker, which theories suggest give some entities the energy they need to be heard. When this occurs you will sometimes hear voices or sounds coming through the static in an attempt to communicate. These voices and sounds are part of radio broadcasts, either AM or FM, and it is suggested by parapsychologists that entities have the ability to direct which words are selected from the many available broadcasts, giving them the ability to control what messages come through the Spirit Box.

2. Ovilus Series I through V

The Ovilus, or Puck, is an electronic speech-synthesis device which uses a speaker to throw out words using a variety of environmental cues. The device was first designed and created by Bill Chappell, a retired electronics engineer with a strong interest in the paranormal field.

The first Ovilus Device had seven modes of operation. It featured a built-in 512-word list as well as a full phonetic generator for ITC experimentation. It used only EMF readings to generate those words through a speaker that could be plugged in to the unit.

The Ovilus FX was next off the production line, containing a word list double that of the Ovilus I. It also had the ability to replay the last thousand words that came through, and had a built-in speaker for ease of use.

Many co-devices and add-ons for the early Ovilus units followed, giving investigators the ability to run the devices independently during an investigation yet also allowing the units to be plugged into a computer for further analysis of results. Other additions with plug-in capability to the Ovilus allowed digital display of the words received on the Ovilus.

The Ovilus II and other devices afterwards added the ability to plug in video goggles to the devices, and were manufactured in limited runs as per demand.

From the maker's website, the odds of actually getting a response from an entity that is related to the question asked, are one of the following:

1:512 (Ovilus I), 1:1024 (Ovilus FX/Video Ovilus), 1:2048 (PX), or 1:2048+,- (Ovilus II/Ovilus X, due to their user-changeable dictionaries).

There are anywhere from 512 words to over 2048 in the database, depending on the type of Ovilus being used, which gives you some idea of the complexity of the possible results, especially in the later models.

We use Ovilus V, the latest incarnation from the manufacturer. This device has both a speaker and a digital screen for results, and a number of environmental options for driving those results, but we mainly use the dictionary mode, as other devices cover the other environmental cue readings. The Ovilus V uses many different environmental cues to draw words from its on-board dictionary, and seems to have a learning period, where the entities at any one place learn more over time on how to utilise the environment to say what they want to put forward.

I wasn't really a massive fan of the Ovilus devices when I first used them a few years before we started our Beechworth tours, but we decided to get the equipment to supplement the many pieces of kit we had for our tours. Then, the devices arrived, and I opened one up and turned it on. The fourth word that came out of the newly-opened Ovilus was my wife's name. Too precise to be a coincidence, I thought. So I set the device down on the table to go and tell my wife about that response, and three more words appeared on the screen and came through the speaker.

"List, things, today," were the three words. The Ovilus was sitting on a list of things for shopping I had drawn up that morning.

"Well, that's to be expected, in a haunted asylum," you might say.

The thing is, we were at home in our rented house when this happened. The house itself was over 100 years old, and was the original firehouse for Beechworth. Being an 1800s goldfield, the whole town is, of course, fairly haunted.

THE INVESTIGATION

C onducting a paranormal investigation can be as individual as you like. There are very few hard and fast rules, but the basics should be the same across the board.

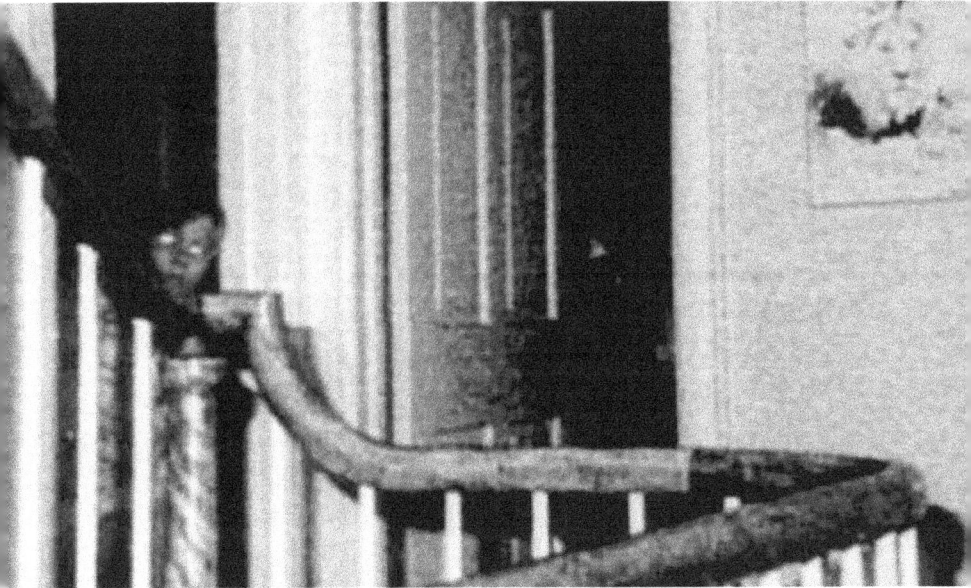

This creepy image was allegedly captured in the infamous Amityville house during a 1976 investigation led by paranormal experts Ed and Lorraine Warren. A camera was set up on the second-floor landing to shoot black-and-white infrared film throughout the night. Every image was empty of unusual phenomena, save this one. George Lutz, the patriarch at the centre of the Amityville Horror story, revealed the photo on The Merv Griffin Show in 1979 and suggested it may show the ghost of John deFeo, a young boy who was murdered in the house before the Lutz family moved in.

The authenticity of the photo, along with the Amityville story, has been widely doubted, with some holding that the photo depicts Paul Bartz, who was part of the Warrens' investigation team.

As stated earlier, research, legalities, and safety should be paramount for all investigators. I'll repeat a few of those points here, due to them being of predominant importance to ensure the industry gains some level of validity.

First off, let's look at what *not* to do.

Don't break in. Don't trespass. Don't destroy.

There seems to be a concept with some people that so long as you can gain entry, by whatever means necessary, to what appears to be an abandoned, possibly-haunted property near you, you have every right to be there. That is not the case.

It's this sort of thinking that damages the industry, and makes us all look bad.

A perfect example of this is the recent destruction of a historic property in the southern United States in late 2013. The LeBeau Plantation house near the Mississippi River in Louisiana was destroyed beyond repair as the result of some foolish people deciding to go ghost-hunting and ended up setting fire to the property.

It's fine to have fun, but please, show some intelligence and have respect for our heritage. Old places can't be replaced.

Don't go into abandoned places on your own. Between the dangers of run-down or potentially-risky structural integrity and the risk of other people who may not be friendly, there are many ways to be hurt when exploring. If you are on your own, you increase the risks associated with these kinds of adventures.

Don't go anywhere, even as a group, without letting others know where you intend to be. Haven't you all seen that movie? We have. It never ends well.

Don't go drunk or drug-affected. This removes any level of sensible behaviour you may usually exhibit, increasing the risk to you, your group, and the facility you are in. It also reduces your ability to run a reasonable, logical investigation.

Basically, respect is essential. Respect for yourself, for others, for the equipment you use, for the scientific or spiritual process, and finally for the places you go and the spirits who remain in them.

Check the power and battery situation in your para-case. Be

prepared. Go to the toilet before you leave for the investigation (let's face it, old places rarely have working toilets, and there is nothing like thinking you've smelt a ghost when in fact someone has gone to the toilet upstairs). Take water and snacks along in case you have something happen that keeps you there longer than you planned. Wear safe and comfortable clothing and footwear.

THE PROCESS OF INVESTIGATION

Everyone has different ideas on what makes a good, respectful investigation. This is ours.

First, do what research you can on the location. Known entities (if any, and really, never trust town legends or anything you find on the Internet). Check government records if the facility is likely to have them. Find out information on previous occupants. Know what you might find.

During an investigation, a series of experiments are undertaken, with the hoped-for outcome of results that show interaction with spirits.

ALWAYS try to link the equipment to the potential for spirits/ hauntings… for example, our basic meter, the Ghost Meter Pro which is handed out to customers, reads electromotive force (EMF), which is the net electric potential ("voltage") thrown out by all living beings. The theory that connects this to spirits is the belief that when passing over, the life energy of the person can't be dispersed, so if a spirit remains, that same EMF will still appear and the entity uses that energy to interact with us. This same theory carries over to EMF pumps where adding to the EMF strength of an area will allow the spirits to use that extra energy to manifest easier and more strongly, yet still in obviously unusual and (hopefully) intelligent ways.

When you first arrive, take baseline measurements with all your equipment. If you are setting up cameras and/or other equipment throughout the location, make careful notes as to what is where, so you can make sure you retrieve it all when you go. The stuff is expensive.

Have a plan in place regarding how you intend to investigate, and if you split up, make sure you are always aware of where everyone else is to avoid contamination of results. Nothing is quite so embarrassing as finding out that wonderful EVP is another group member cursing under their breath while looking for a working toilet.

Some basic fundamentals:

Be patient. These things can take time to get any result at all. Spirits can take a while to come forward, and can take time to learn how to interact with the equipment itself through environmental control.

Be open-minded. There are no 'set' styles of doing this. Be aware that even if there were set ways, the spirits themselves may not be aware of this. You are dealing with people.

Be courteous and respectful. Would you engage with someone who was being rude or demanding? Some may, but others may not. We've always found respectful dialogue gets the best results, and we require that within our own facility.

Be open to using new techniques with equipment. Just because something is meant to be used one way doesn't mean it won't work another way. Experimentation and innovation are the keys.

Try and make the questions you may ask answerable with YES/NO (closed questions) for the simpler equipment, and only use open questions where you have the equipment to take those answers.

Try to remember that spirits you may encounter may be of a different time, so try to keep the questions relevant and easily-understood. Don't refer to things that may not be known in the past.

KNOWN SPIRITS WITHIN MAYDAY HILLS

N aming Information – Beechworth Lunatic Asylum (1867–1905); Hospital for the Insane (1905–34); Mental Hospital (1934–c.96); Beechworth Psychiatric Hospital, known as Mayday Hills (1977–c.96); Beechworth Training Centre (1964–95).

The asylum was built between 1864-67 and opened in October 1867.

After 128 years of operation, it closed in 1995. During that operating period, there were over 9,000 recorded deaths.

The original asylum buildings took 200 workers four years to complete. Many of the labourers were prisoners from the Beechworth Gaol serving hard-labour time. The asylum grounds covered 200 acres, although it now covers less than 50 acres. Beechworth Asylum was self-sufficient in nearly every way. The only resource regularly brought in was soap, usually carbolic soap made by residents of Kew's Willsmere Asylum and shipped out to other government facilities in Victoria.

Originally, stable and biddable patients worked in the gardens, orchards, farm, sewing room, laundry and kitchen for their keep. Later, roughly the middle of the 20th century, they were paid for their labour before all work stopped in the asylum due to OH & S regulations, likely around the late 20th century. Originally, all light and heating was candle, kerosene, coal and wood, with electricity connected in 1926.

General Paranormal Activity throughout the facility can include (but certainly isn't limited to) nausea, dizziness, odours, headaches, aches and pains, light touches and pulling of hair, whispers and faint voices, shadows and orbs (really only relevant when seen with the naked eye. There are also occasional examples of stones and other small objects being thrown or moved).

BIJOU THEATRE COMPLEX

The main central recreation hall is now known as the Bijou Theatre hall and Store. This is comprised of the Bijou Hall itself, the staff reading rooms ('Blue Room') behind the stage, the Billiard Room (upstairs) which is now used by Mayday Escape Rooms, the Bell Tower (now removed and taken back to roof level, although the access stairs still partially remain), the original kitchen (the ghost tours and theatre foyer), and the mezzanine area and the projection box (1940s) above the foyer.

There are many entities known to inhabit the main hall of the asylum. Here are a few we have so far interacted with and found (alleged) names for.

- Tommy (Kennedy?) in foyer – Reputed to be a red-haired Irish larrikin, Tommy has been known since before our tours started. Rumoured to be a patient from the 1930s, Tommy is supposed to have passed as a result of a spilt vat of boiling liquid when he slipped in the kitchen (now the foyer) and grabbed for support to stop falling over, pulling the vat over onto him. Legend says he was a multi-tasking worker, making himself useful as a deliveryman and kitchenhand, as well as helping transport bodies from the main area to the morgue. Tommy is a practical joker, regularly poking guests and making himself known, and has been seen to play with technology like mobile phones and such when left unattended.

- "Unknown doppelganger" – Multiple times one of our staff has seen another staff member appear as a completely solid apparition when they could not possibly be there due to not even being present at the asylum or are out on tours. This has happened at least 3-4 times in the four years we've been running the tours.
- Ralph (Projection Box & mezzanine) – projectionist. Projection Box still houses two projectors.
- Young Girl (Hall) – Tugs on ladies' clothing, usually around the double entry doors from the foyer. Believed to be non-English speaking.
- Lady playing a piano (Hall) – It is believed that a catatonic patient would be brought over to play the piano for the cinema. She would be placed in front of the piano and once the film started, she would play. When the film finished, she would lapse back into her catatonic state. Since we placed an old piano down near the stage, playing has been heard on occasion.
- Thomas (Bell Tower Window) – Middle window, above the stage. Hall Porter responsible for the ringing the bell for shift changes.

THE BIRCHES (ADMINISTRATION BUILDING)

The main front building of the asylum, this was designed in what is known as Italianate style – influenced by buildings from the Italian Renaissance. This building originally housed the superintendent, the surgeons, surgeries, and administration areas. The second floor had been leased by Beechworth Day Spa since before any tours ran through the facility, but with our

access now we are the first to be able to investigate this area.

The ghosts who inhabit this area are:

- William, the first patient to die in the asylum, only a day or two after opening.
- Lady seen in second floor (LHS) window – believed to have died in the 1960s, rumoured to have either suicided or to have been pushed out of the window in an argument over a

packet of cigarettes.

- Lisa, a young girl on the second floor, who regularly appears within a small confinement or storage room where it was rumoured she died after being locked in as punishment by one of the administrators and then forgotten when the family took a trip to Melbourne for a holiday.

DOUBLE-STORY PHARMACY

This area was once part of the men's side, but was adapted to an office area and pharmacy after the fire in 1951.

Known activity within this space:

- Robert, who we first encountered in the downstairs pharmacy, but since moved upstairs. Also encountered in admin, top floor.

- Black Blobby Thing: first here, then followed us to Grevillea. Initially described as a black blob (hence the name we still use), this spirit gradually became more coherent as time went on. When he came through it was strong and uncomfortable for the group. He first came through in the pharmacy in Robert's room as two people saw him in the scullery and he would not let Robert interact with us. The description fits in with what Carina, myself, and a few guests saw on one overnighter in Grevillea. He was later described as a tall, solid and a grubby person. We're not sure if he is staff or a patient as we could not get a definite yes or no.

THE BULLPIT (MEN'S WING)

This north-south extension added on to the east-west male wing was built in 1870s, soon after the opening of the asylum when the government realised there were a lot more beds needed than was originally planned. It was initially used as a ward for young men (from late teens to mid-twenties, we think).

Entities suspected to inhabit this area are:

- Young boy (back verandah) – often seen playing around the trees and verandah posts. It is believed he used to scavenge for food at the asylum due to being from a poor local family.
- Arthur (seen walking between the Store and the Bull Pit) – It is believed this gentleman worked in the veggie garden. He was known to always wear a heavy green jacket both summer and winter. When he died, 140 pounds was found stashed in the lining of his coat.

THE CELLAR

Prisoners were often locked in the cells behind the metal gates instead of returning to the gaol each night and then coming back up the hill in the morning, which would make sense and gain an extra two hours' work out the men.

There have been instances of legs and ankles being touched, shadows moving near the groups, and even a visual of someone standing in doorways, a feeling of being suffocated, and even scratching (usually teenage boys).

Ghosts of the cellar may include:

- A man seen standing behind the metal gate or at the bottom of the stairs.
- Colin – a prisoner believed to be both deaf and dumb, and responsible for the rare times a teeneage boy receives some scratches..

FEMALE COURTYARD

This area was known as the female airing yard, as patients would be brought out for air. It is known that at one point there was a tennis court situated here.

Ghosts regularly sighted in this courtyard are:

- Rex – used to play tennis by himself without a racquet or balls. A chain smoker.
- A woman in white.
- A man in a top hat (School of Nursing verandah).

MALE COURTYARD

The airing yard on this side of the hall once held bowling and croquet greens, as well as being the airing yard for the male prisoners.

Ghosts sighted in this area are:

- Man in top hat (tree in round-about between men's ward/Toy Shop and kiosk).

GREVILLEA/HOPSITAL WARD

Grevillea was originally two smaller fourteen-bed male cottages later joined to form the Male Infirmary. Once the gender division within the hospital was relaxed, it became a general hospital ward for either gender. Approximately 3,000 patients died in this building alone, and activity level within Grevillea certainly reflects that.

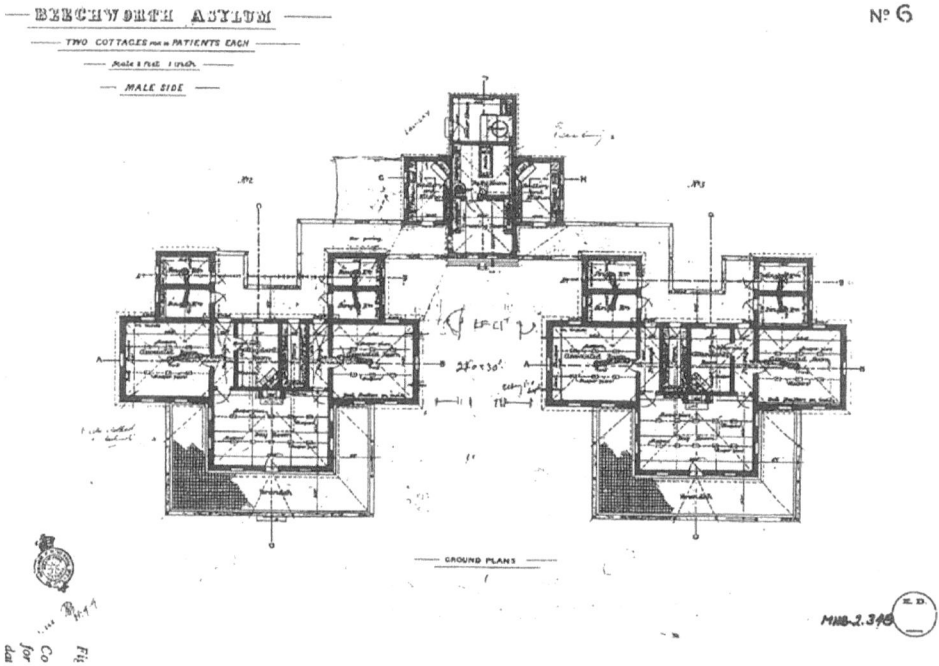

Activity regularly experienced includes: scratching sometimes heard coming from one of the cells that lead from the room with the morgue table, doors banging, footsteps, and other noises that may or may not be paranormal.
- Ghosts we regularly encounter in Grevillea:
- Girl/small lady at the far end of the main room.
- Man at the end of the corridor leading to the morgue table. He sometimes comes further forward, almost into the morgue table room.

- Nurse (solitary treatment room) – the night before a patient was to receive ECT (Electro Convulsive Therapy) nursing staff would report seeing a nurse (in old-style uniform) sitting on the patient's bed, or of the room being so cold they could see their own breath.
- Benjamin/Carlisle – two entities we first encountered in the 70s kitchen, until that building was used for a storage company and we stopped taking tours in there. A month or so later, these two started interacting in Grevillea, so we can only assume they followed so they could continue to engage with the groups. Benjamin appears to be a small boy around ten years old, and Carlisle is a massive, looming man who seems to be Benjamin's guardian or companion.

LAUNDRY

The laundry is an imposing area within a facility that is already impressive. Three stories tall, it looms over you once you enter. For me, I always think of the old Addam's Family home, from the shape of the windows and the shape of the ceiling as it swoops up to form a ventilation lantern like the feature in foyer, but larger.

Over the years, many patients and staff worked in the laundry section. Washing, drying, ironing, folding and storage of clothes, linen and blankets… all done here in the laundry. You can only imagine the workload and the steam and heat.

This area is one of the more fear-inducing regions of the asylum. This is where we saw (and filmed) a piece of paranormal equipment slide on the floor by itself.

Known ghosts within the laundry area:

- Paul and Mary are two spirits linked by tragedy. Paul was reportedly a delivery driver who used to assault Mary (a laundry worker, but we're unsure if she was staff or patient) when delivering to the laundry. From rumour, he murdered her and was then committed to the asylum as a patient. Paul's presence is dark, and can be quite powerful at times. He has been known to touch female guests, and pull hair, especially that of young, blonde patrons. Mary is more withdrawn and either holds back most contact or is held back by Paul, the stronger spirit. During one of our livefeeds, we had equipment move by itself, and Mary has taken credit for this manifestation of energy.

UPPER WOMEN'S WARD/MANIACAL WARD

This ward is an original 1860s building that has undergone very few changes and renovations. Originally built with three separate sections, it now all links together (at least on the top floor) to form one long ward and workhouse section. This wing was closed in the mid-1970s and used as storage for many years, which explains why it was never renovated or updated.

The top floor holds four original 1860s cells in the ward section, as well as the Matron's apartment and office area in the middle section and the Sewing Room at the east end. Originally, the Matron's area was separated from both the ward area and

the sewing room/work area but later, the two areas that held the earth closet and the water closet were opened up to form doorways to the east and west of the Matron's area. We think this occurred sometime after the 1940s, but we can't be sure at this point. By then, Matron was already moved from this building to an apartment in the main admin building, and from there to the Nurses' Hostel (now Linaker Hotel) later on.

One of the original matrons (we think it is Matron Sharpe, from the late 1800s) is still regularly encountered in this area, and is also known to move throughout the rest of the hospital.

Other ghosts we have come across in this area:

- Nurse Kate Cavanagh – First Female Warder. Sometimes a light is seen travelling across the windows. It is thought to be Nurse Cavanagh doing her rounds. In the past, while the hospital was still functioning, night staff (who had fallen asleep on duty) have reported being woken by a nurse in an old-style nursing uniform.
- Lizzie (cell with bedframe) and Maggie occupy the two cells either side of the fireplace on the top floor. Both are very chatty at times, and happy to interact with the groups.

LOWER WOMEN'S WARD/MANIACAL WARD

The lower floor is similar (but not quite the same toward the east end) as the upper, with another four original 1860s cells in similar condition to the upper floor. The day room outside the cells was in much worse condition, with a weakened floor, which on investigation was found to be a layer of linoleum over the joists with no boards at all, and the solid plastering on the ceiling was weakened and dropping in places. We recently went through and made the area safer so we could offer a tour of the ground floor. An old wooden staircase (not safe for groups to use as far as we can tell) leads up to the matron's area, and the lower floor has no through corridor to the laundry wing. We believe the area directly below Matron's was originally used to house the senior seamstress, and one of the rooms has what we call a light tunnel leading directly to the attic, with areas that are open at the top for what we think was to lower the buckets containing night soil (sewerage) to the collection point below for disposal. The separate laundry at the east end is covered above.

Known ghosts in this area:
- Will is the only name we have unique to this area, and he was believed to have been a delivery man for the laundry and seamstresses. He is often seen as a shadow figure just outside the door to the lower area, and has been known to play with shoelaces of guides and guests.
- Matron Sharpe is also regularly seen in this area.

OLIVENE (HIGH SECURITY MALE WARD)

Olivene, the men's criminally insane cottage and high security area for males, was part of the hospital expansion in the 1890s. It was built to house twenty-two people, with cell areas off the open courtyard for the more dangerous patients.

The large table currently inhabiting the main dayroom area comes from a railway station and is owned by the Burke Museum. We can't be sure if it is ever able to be moved out of the building due to its massive size, so it may well be there forever.

Activity within this building can be common among guides and guests, including but not limited to burning sensations, as well as sudden headaches and general uneasiness, both of which can just as suddenly disappear once the group leaves Olivene. Common occurrences can include banging or tapping on walls, doors, or the table, a suddenly-spinning exhaust fan in the ceiling of the main room, which sometimes even spins in the direction asked by paranormal investigation groups, and other less noticeable things like a shadow figure peering from the kitchen into the main room, and sometimes even the figure of someone hanging from the ceiling.

Known ghosts within Olivene:

- Ted occupies the first cell on the left as the group goes into the courtyard. Ted is rumoured to be a giant of a man, at least six foot six, with long hair and beard. He was originally admitted for murdering his barber after an argument about the hair and beard trim he received, so the warders were understandably reluctant to cut his long locks while he was in here.
- A shadow is sometimes seen walking along the front veranda outside the windows while the group is inside.
- There is a story of a man named Abraham who was murdered by another patient in the main room. A broom was broken over his head and he subsequently fell into the open fireplace and died three days later from burns and bleeding on the brain. Sometimes guests report smelling burnt hair and/or flesh in that area.

SOME EXPERIENCES IN THE ASYLUM

As collected and recorded by Dawn

During the first few months of us taking over the buildings and tours, we experienced a high volume of many kinds of activity. Noises, shadow figures, whispering, doors slamming and locking, almost as though the spirits were testing our resolve, as though we were playthings.

On the night Geoff saw his first apparition, it was only a few months into the first year of operation, and he was still in awe of the facility and running on a hair-trigger of fear. He went over to the women's maniacal ward to lock the door after the tour had left the building (we didn't have the best locking set-up in our early days, and we had to unlock and relock after the tour went through areas) and as he opened the door to then use that space to pull it closed, he swears he saw a hand beckoning with a single finger to come inside. He slammed the door and ran screaming back to the foyer.

Another visual sighting happened around the same time, when Geoff was going over to the Toy Shop (no longer on the tour route) and he saw what appeared to be a tall gentleman in a full black suit, waistcoat and top hat. It was all very clear, even down to the moonlight shining on the brass buttons of the waistcoat. The only thing in full shadow was the gentleman's face. This figure stood under a tree, then vanished after a few seconds. Geoff saw the same figure again when checking the door into the women's ward, before it again vanished quickly after giving what appeared to be a short nod to Geoff. The third and final time this figure was sighted was by the tour guide after the group had returned from the tour and subsequently left the asylum. The guide went outside for a cigarette, and screamed. Geoff heard this from the foyer, rushed out, and saw the same figure walking the veranda of the women's area. He turned to the guide, asked what was wrong, and the guide described seeing the exact same figure Geoff had seen, without being told what the figure looked like.

Sometimes, entire periods of activity occur, usually related to an anniversary (most active time of the year is every October, an anniversary of the opening of the facility) or a geomagnetic event. An example is outlined below.

Abnormal Geomagnetic event November 2-5th 2018

According to Wiki, "A geomagnetic storm (commonly referred to as a solar storm) is a temporary disturbance of the Earth's magnetosphere caused by a solar wind shock wave and/or cloud of magnetic field that interacts with the Earth's magnetic field." As we believe that spirits tap into that kind of energy to materialise, it makes sense to us that activity during solar storms would ramp up exponentially.

We had a strong geomagnetic event at the end of August of 2018 with a rise of activity during this time, but the event of November of that year was especially active up here.

This geomagnetic event supplied quite a few experiences, especially during the 3rd and 4th of the month, for patrons of the asylum and of Beechworth in general.

---SATURDAY AFTERNOON---

1 – Two staff were on the top floor of the women's ward working on a new display when they both saw a shadow cross from right to left of a corridor. This was during broad daylight. No one else was in the building. After that, the two went to another section and started discussing that area. One stepped into a room, then stepped out and they chatted a bit more. She stepped back into that room and she said that the vibe of the

room had changed to "not very nice". The other started feeling like she had butterflies in the tummy, then felt like she was going to be sick, so they went out. As they were going down the steps to the ground floor, it felt like a nice breeze was blowing all those feelings away.

2 – About thirty minutes later in the same building, Geoff took an artefact over to the new display area we were setting up. He left the trolley at the bottom of the stairs, and took the artefact upstairs to place it. While he was upstairs he heard the trolley wheels rolling. When he went back downstairs, he found the trolley had been turned around a full 180-degrees to face the other way. Now, there is a tiny bit of wave to the floor it was sitting on, so it's not entirely level, but that should NOT have been possible.

---SATURDAY NIGHT---

1 – Guide had a couple standing with the group at the autopsy table and yet clearly saw them at the barber chair in the other room. A young girl also saw it yet the group verified the couple hadn't wandered off. Also, a chair was heard being dragged along the floor in the female sewing room area, and heard by the whole group.

2 – Customer fainted tonight in exactly the same place another customer had a blood nose a couple of days ago (guide was just talking about lobotomies when the nose started bleeding). BOTH customers said these events were NOT usual for them.

3 – Two doors were opened and closed by themselves throughout the tours tonight. On one tour, a door was open (impossible because it has a bolt holding it closed) and then for the next tour it was closed again. All this was on top of our normal level of activity.

4 – The manager was running the foyer and said the level of noise and footsteps and such in the hall was astounding.

---SUNDAY AFTERNOON---

1 – Geoff got a phone call from a woman asking if the town has

any costumed people wandering around at night. Her husband was in town (in the main street) at around 2am the night before, and saw a woman in a long, white, old-fashioned dress with long sleeves and a white cap. From photos they looked up this morning, it looked like an old nurse's or matron's get-up. The 'person' walked past the front of Tanswell's Commercial Hotel and then turned down a laneway beside it. He went to look into the lane and no-one was there.

2 – Timmy (one of the escape rooms' owners) was exiting the building through the door that leads to outside near the Kiosk. He was closing the door, and it was suddenly pushed closed fast and hard from inside, to the point where it slammed loudly. No-one was inside at the door to do so.

---SUNDAY NIGHT---

A great tour tonight.

1 – We had four people leave the tour early, two separate groups of two, each stating the whole place was way too energised for them, and it was too overwhelming.

2 – Another guy went to the car to get money to buy a book at the end of the tour, and the car unlocked itself before he even got there. The key was in his pocket, yet as he approached, the lights flashed and car unlocked. He did not have a key with keyless entry. This has happened before, but not for a while.

AFTERWORD

So ends this short introduction to the asylum and its inhabitants, along with some basics covering the techniques and thoughts on investigating the paranormal.

We started Asylum Ghost Tours just over four years ago, and in that time we've been up here a lot, both day and night. Although I tend to debunk everything that occurs, I have personally witnessed and experienced a lot of things I can't debunk. I certainly believe there are things here that modern science is yet to explain.

All I can say is that the paranormal and supernatural things that can be experienced are subjective: people can tell you a million times of things they have witnessed, but until you experience something yourself, you just won't believe.

In the end, what we have up here at Mayday Hills is something very special, whether you're interested in history, spirits, or the two combined.

Come visit, stay a while. After all, it's only a decommissioned asylum... what could possibly go wrong?

Geoff Brown, March 2020. Still virus free.

ASYLUM
GHOST TOURS
BEECHWORTH, VICTORIA
0473 376 848
WWW.ASYLUMGHOSTTOURS.COM